Let's Discover The States

Eastern Great Lakes

INDIANA • MICHIGAN • OHIO

By
Thomas G. Aylesworth
Virginia L. Aylesworth

CHELSEA HOUSE PUBLISHERS
New York   Philadelphia

Created and produced by Blackbirch Graphics, Inc.

DESIGN: Richard S. Glassman
PROJECT EDITOR: Bruce S. Glassman
ASSOCIATE EDITOR: Robin Langley Sommer

3   5   7   9   8   6   4
Printed in the United States

Library of Congress Cataloging-in-Publication Data

Aylesworth, Thomas G.
    Eastern Great Lakes: Indiana, Michigan, Ohio

    (Let's discover the states)
    Includes bibliographies and index.
    Summary: Discusses the geographical, historical, and cultural aspects of Ohio, Indiana, and Michigan.
    1. Lakes States—Juvenile literature.   2. Ohio—Juvenile literature.   3. Indiana—Juvenile literature.
4. Michigan—Juvenile literature.   [1. Lakes States.   2. Ohio.   3. Indiana.   4. Michigan]   I. Aylesworth,
Virginia L.   II. Title.   III. Series: Aylesworth, Thomas G. Let's discover the states.
F551.A95 1988   977   87-17877
ISBN 1-55546-559-5
    0-7910-0534-8 (pbk.)

CONTENTS

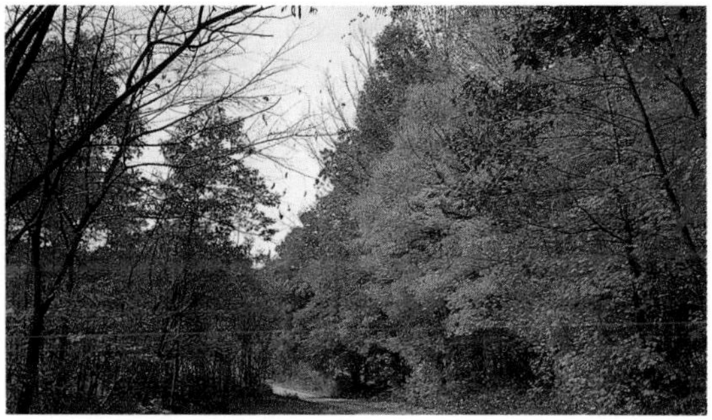

Sunset casting its glow on the waters of the Ohio River near Madison.

Thousands of cheering basketball fans in Assembly Hall in Bloomington.

The serenity of the beech- and pine-shaded trails in McCormick's Creek State Park.

The beautiful Grotto of Our Lady of Lourdes on the Notre Dame campus in South Bend.

Engines roaring as competitors circle the track in the Indy 500.

Rows of white sand dunes bordering mighty Lake Michigan.

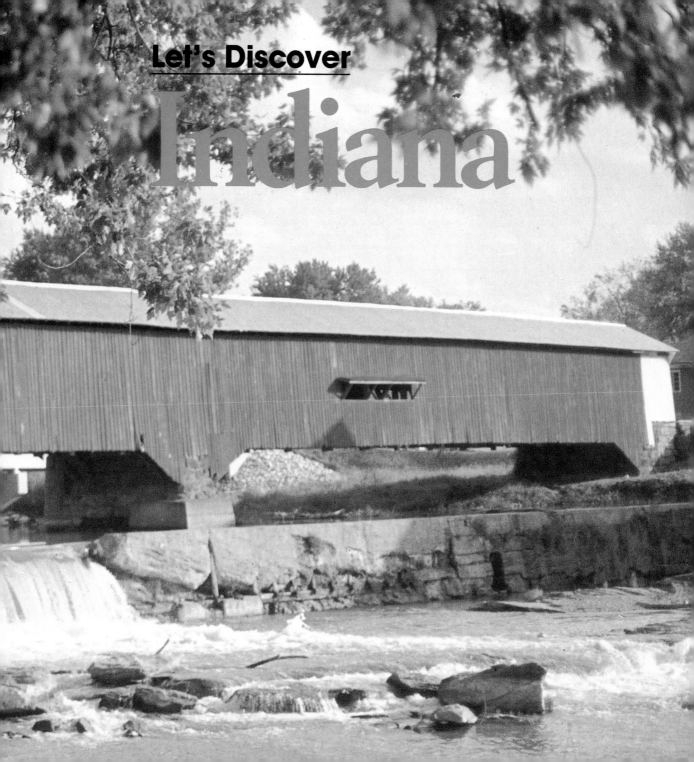

Let's Discover

Indiana

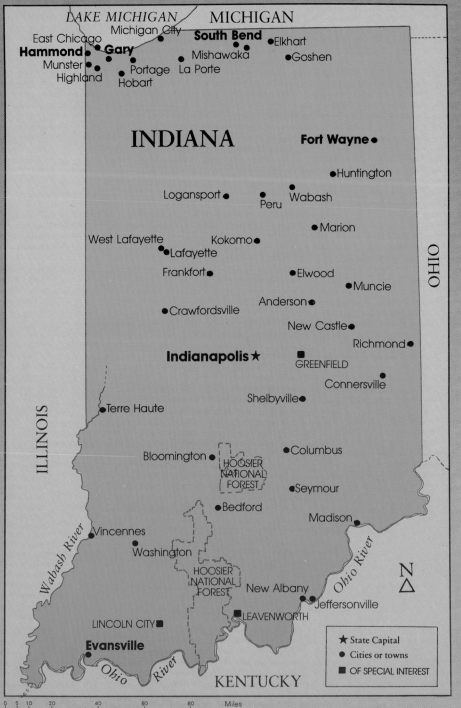

LAKE MICHIGAN   MICHIGAN

East Chicago   Michigan City   **South Bend**
Hammond   **Gary**   ●Elkhart
Munster   Mishawaka   ●Goshen
Highland   Portage   La Porte
Hobart

INDIANA

Fort Wayne ●

●Huntington

Logansport ●   ●   Wabash
Peru

●Marion

West Lafayette   Kokomo ●
●Lafayette

Frankfort●   ●Elwood
●Muncie

Anderson●

●Crawfordsville   New Castle●
Richmond●

Indianapolis ★   ■
GREENFIELD   Connersville●

Shelbyville●

●Columbus
Bloomington●   HOOSIER
NATIONAL
FOREST   ●Seymour
●Bedford

Madison●
●Terre Haute

Vincennes●
Washington●   HOOSIER
NATIONAL
FOREST   New Albany●
Jeffersonville●

LINCOLN CITY ■   ■LEAVENWORTH

Evansville●

Wabash River   Ohio River

ILLINOIS

OHIO

KENTUCKY

Ohio River

N
△

★ State Capital
● Cities or towns
■ OF SPECIAL INTEREST

0 5 10   20   40   60   80   Miles
0 5 10 20   40   60   80   100   120   140   Kilometres

State Bird: Cardinal

State Flower: Peony

State Motto: The
Crossroads of America

State Tree: Tulip Tree

Nickname: Hoosier State

INDIANA
At a Glance

Capital: Indianapolis

Major Industries: Metals, transportation equipment, electronics

Major Crops: Corn, soybeans, wheat, hay

Size: 36,291 square miles (38th largest)

Population: 5,498,000 (14th largest)

State Flag

The Land

Indiana is bounded on the west by Illinois, on the north by Michigan and Lake Michigan, on the east by Ohio, and on the south by Kentucky. There are three main land regions in the state. From north to south, they are the Great Lakes Plains, the Till Plains, and the Southern Hills and Lowlands.

The Great Lakes Plains, sometimes called the Northern Lake and Moraine Region, are part of a larger area of fertile lowlands along the shoreline of the Great Lakes. Here sand dunes rim Lake Michigan, with farmlands of dark, rich soil to the south. The farmers of the region raise beef cattle, soybeans, potatoes, poultry, vegetables, and corn.

The Till Plains of central Indiana, composed of soil and other materials (till) deposited during the Ice Age, are part of the great Midwestern Corn Belt. Low hills dot the region, which includes, in Wayne county, the highest point in the state—1,257 feet above sea level. The Till Plains produce fruit, corn, soybeans, and vegetables. Livestock graze on the region's pastures.

Farming is important to Indiana's economy. The state's rich soil and moderate climate make it one of the nation's leading agricultural areas.

Northeastern Indiana is part of the Great Lakes Plains, which consist of fertile lowlands with dark, rich soil. Major lakes in this region include Lakes Wawasee and Manitou and Turkey Lake.

The Southern Hills and Lowlands are the hilliest part of Indiana. This area was untouched by the ancient glaciers. It is a land of limestone caves and steep hills, called knobs. Here are limestone quarries, coal mines, and petroleum wells. Crops grown here include hay, tobacco, wheat, barley, corn, and fruit. Hogs, poultry, and beef and dairy cattle are also raised in the area.

Indiana's most important rivers include the Wabash, the White, the Tippecanoe, the St. Joseph, and the Salamonie. The state has about 36 sizable lakes, of which Lake Wawasee, in the northeast, is the largest. Manitou, Maxinkuckee, and Turkey Lakes are also in northeastern Indiana.

The climate of Indiana is marked by sharply defined seasons and sometimes sudden weather changes. Rainfall, spread throughout the year, averages about 40 inches. Winter temperatures range from about 29 degrees Fahrenheit in the north to 35 degrees F. in the south, although zero-degree weather and heavy snowfalls are not uncommon. Summer averages range from 73 to 86 degrees F. and temperatures over 100 degrees F. have been recorded. Humidity is often high.

Southern Indiana is the hilliest part of the state. This mineral-rich area has coal mines, oil wells, and limestone caves.

The History

About 3,000 years ago, the people who lived in what would become Indiana began to cultivate tobacco and food plants, including sunflower, gourds, squash, and corn. They made pottery and objects carved from sandstone, and constructed huge mounds of earth in which they buried their dead. We know them as the Adena people. Later groups such as the Hopewell built even larger earth mounds that served as fortified villages and ritual areas. Some of these can still be seen. But by the time the Europeans arrived in the 17th century, there were only a few hundred Indians in the territory, primarily members of the Miami tribe, some of whom remain to this day.

During the 1700s and 1800s, Indians from the east came into the area as their lands were taken over by white settlers. These included the Delaware, Mahican, Munsee, and Shawnee. Still others came from the northern Great Lakes region. Among them were the Huron, Kickapoo, Piankashaw, Potawatomi, and Wea tribes. The Potawatomi were the last to enter and the last to leave Indiana; most of them were induced to sell their land to the U.S. government, and others were evicted by military force in 1838. But some Potawatomi remain near South Bend.

The first Europeans to visit the region were probably the Jesuit missionary Jacques Marquette and his companion, Louis Joliet, who traveled through northern Indiana and preached to the Indians in 1673. In 1679 came the French explorer Robert Cavelier, known as La Salle. He started out from French Canada in search of a water route to the Pacific Ocean and traveled down the St. Joseph and Kankakee Rivers. La Salle returned to the region in 1680, reinforcing the French claim to Indiana. French fur traders from Canada came to offer beads, blankets, knives, and whiskey to the Indians in exchange for animal furs. They established trading posts at Miami, near

Fort Wayne was originally the site of a trading post built by the French who protected their trade route between Montreal, Canada and New Orleans, Louisiana, with a series of stockades during the 1700s. The first European settlements grew up along this route.

present-day Fort Wayne, and at Ouiatenon, where Lafayette is today. About 1731 the first permanent white settlement in Indiana was established by the French at Vincennes; a fort was built there two years later.

British fur traders also came into Indiana and clashed with the French. The French claimed the territory because of La Salle's explorations, and the British claimed it as an extension of their Atlantic Seaboard colonies. When the French and Indian Wars broke out, the British finally defeated the French, who gave up their claim to Indiana and other North American holdings in 1763. The French left few marks on the land except for the names of such cities as Vincennes, Terre Haute, and La Porte.

During the Revolutionary War, British troops began to occupy the region. They moved into Vincennes in 1777 and took control of Fort Sackville. In 1778 the American leader George Rogers Clark captured the fort with Virginia frontiersmen and claimed southern Indiana for the state of Virginia. The British recaptured the outpost, but Clark seized it again in 1779. However, faraway Virginia was unable to control the region, and Indiana became public domain in 1784. It was made part of the Northwest Territory in 1787.

Fort Vincennes guarded the French settlement of Vincennes, founded about 1731. It was Indiana's first European settlement.

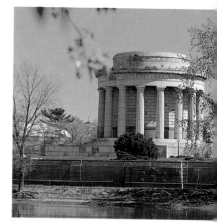

Settlers from the east began to filter in after the Revolution ended in 1783, traveling down the Ohio River (now Indiana's southern boundary) and across Kentucky in what would become a steady stream. Many were former soldiers who held land grants from the government that it had issued instead of back pay. They cleared fields, built settlements, and lived in log cabins. One pioneer couple named Lincoln had come from Kentucky with their young son, Abraham. Soon after they arrived, the mother, Nancy Hanks Lincoln, died, and the boy Abraham helped his father bury her in the forest. It was during the pioneer era that Indiana got its future nickname of the Hoosier State, perhaps from the regional greeting to visitors, "Who's here?"

The Miami Indians, under the leadership of Chief Little Turtle, resisted white encroachments on their land. Aided by the British, Little Turtle and his forces successfully fought off attacks by U.S. government troops in 1790 and 1791. However, in 1794 federal troops under General Anthony Wayne defeated the Miami and allied tribes in the Battle of Fallen Timbers, near present-day Toledo, Ohio.

The Indiana Territory, created in 1800, included what is now Indiana, Illinois, Wisconsin, and parts of Michigan and Minnesota. President John Adams appointed General William Henry Harrison, who was later to be president himself, the territorial governor, with his capital at Vincennes.

Continuing pressure on the Indians by the federal government in Washington and by white settlers led the great Shawnee chief Tecumseh to form a Confederation of Indian Nations that would extend from the Great Lakes to the Gulf of Mexico. While Tecumseh was away gathering support in the south in 1811, Harrison defeated the Indians in the Battle of Tippecanoe, near present-day Lafayette. This dealt a fatal blow to the Indian organization.

The Indians then joined British forces against the Americans in the War of 1812, but federal troops and militia burned their towns and granaries. The Indians stood with the British in a last furious attempt to defend their land, but Tecumseh's death in the Battle of the

William Henry Harrison became the first governor of the Indiana Territory when it was created in 1800, with Vincennes as its capital. Conflict with the Indians over land rights culminated in the 1811 Battle of Tippecanoe, in which Harrison defeated the confederation led by Shawnee chief Tecumseh.

Thames River in Canada two years later marked the end of their resistance in Indiana. Corydon became the new capital of the Indiana Territory in 1813. Settlers began to pour in, including thousands of immigrants from Europe. Among them were the Swiss, who moved into the forests to do woodworking and make furniture. They named Switzerland County and the river settlement of Tell City. Germans helped develop Terre Haute and Indianapolis, becoming bankers, brewers, and civic leaders.

Indiana joined the Union in 1816 as the 19th state, and in 1821 Indianapolis was named the new state capital. Railroads began pushing into the state in the 1850s and the economy expanded. Farmers had new markets for their crops, and industries for their products. The Studebaker brothers opened their blacksmith and wagon shop in South Bend in 1852, and it was soon the largest

wagon-making factory in the country (later it became an important automobile manufacturer). Richard Gatling had invented the first practical machine gun in Indianapolis in 1862. During the 1860s James Oliver improved the steel plow invented by John Deere to cut through the tough prairie land.

There was only one battle in Indiana during the Civil War—the Battle of Corydon. John Hunt Morgan, a Confederate cavalry general, led Morgan's Raiders up from Kentucky to raid the former state capital. Then they rode on to Ohio.

Throughout the last half of the 19th century, the character of Indiana changed slowly from rural-agricultural to highly industrialized. One of the first gasoline pumps in the United States was manufactured at Fort Wayne in 1885. Natural gas was discovered near Portland the following year. In 1889 the Standard Oil Company built one of the world's largest oil refineries in the little village of Whiting. In 1894 Elwood Haynes of Kokomo designed one of the first successful gasoline-powered automobiles.

Oliver P. Morton was governor of Indiana during the Civil War era, when the state endured a grave political and financial crisis.

The Kepler House still stands in New Harmony, the experimental community that established the first coeducational school in the United States in 1825.

In 1906 the United States Steel Corporation selected a tract of sand dunes on the south shore of Lake Michigan as the site of a new steel-making city, to be called Gary. The city became the core of a vast industrial complex devoted to steel, iron, and chemicals, stretching 45 miles along the shore of the lake in the great Calumet Region.

The first 500-mile race was held at the Indianapolis Motor Speedway in 1911, attesting to Indiana's confidence in the future of the automobile. Six years later, the United States entered World War I, in which more than 130,000 Indiana men served. After the war, the automobile and metal-products industries expanded, although agriculture remained important to the state's economy.

More than 340,000 men and women from Indiana served in the armed forces during World War II, when the state's steel and fuel were important to the war effort. In the second half of the 20th century, Indiana's location at the crossroads of the nation has made it one of the most typically American states in the Union. Against the still-visible background of Indian history and the determined pioneer struggle for survival, it stands out as a region that has come of age.

Indiana was the first state in the nation to provide in its constitution for a state-wide system of free public education—in 1816. In 1825 the experimental community of New Harmony established the first coeducational school in the United States. The first public library in the state was opened in 1807 in Vincennes. Indiana University, the first institution of higher education, opened in 1820, just four years after statehood. Many others followed. By the beginning of the Civil War in 1861, there were 15 colleges and universities, including Hanover College (1827), Wabash College (1832), Franklin College of Indiana (1834), DePauw University (1837), Concordia Senior College (1839), St. Mary-of-the-Woods College (1840), The University of Notre Dame (1842), St. Mary's College (1844), Taylor University (1846), Earlham College (1847), Evansville College (1854), St. Meinrad Seminary (1854), Butler University (1855), and Valparaiso University (1859).

The University of Notre Dame, in South Bend, is one of the leading Roman Catholic universities in the country.

The world-famous "Indy 500" automobile race is held each year at the Indianapolis Motor Speedway. The 500-mile race is part of an annual event that attracts thousands of visitors during the Memorial Day weekend.

The People

More than 64 percent of the people in Indiana live in towns and cities, including Indianapolis, Fort Wayne, and Evansville, and 98 percent of them were born in the United States. The biggest single religious group in the state consists of Roman Catholics, although the Protestant churches combined have a larger membership. Sizable Protestant denominations include the Baptists, Lutherans, Methodists, Presbyterians, and members of the Disciples of Christ.

Indiana has always been a literary state. Among the great writers who were born there are novelist Theodore Dreiser, the author of *Sister Carrie* and *An American Tragedy* (Terre Haute); journalist and war correspondent Ernie Pyle (Dana); the beloved poet and author of

"The Old Swimmin' Hole," James Whitcomb Riley (Greenfield); the Pulitzer Prize-winning novelist Booth Tarkington, author of the *Penrod* books and *The Magnificent Ambersons* (Indianapolis); and Lew Wallace (Brookville), the author of the monumental *Ben-Hur*.

Civil War general Ambrose Burnside, who led Union forces, was born in Liberty. The social reformer Eugene Debs was from Terre Haute. Basketball superstar Larry Bird is a native of French Lick. Choreographer Twyla Tharp was born in Portland, and talk-show host David Letterman is from Indianapolis. Oddly enough, Midwestern Indiana has been good to the fashion industry, which is centered in New York City. Designer Bill Blass was born in Fort Wayne, Halston (Roy Halston Frowick) grew up in Evansville, and Norell (Norman Levinson) was born in Noblesville.

Many fine actors, actresses, and entertainers have come from the Hoosier State, including James Dean (Marion), Academy Award-winner Anne Baxter (Michigan City), singer Michael Jackson (Gary), Alex Karras (Gary), Shelley Long (Fort Wayne), and Red Skelton (Vincennes).

Astronaut Virgil Ivan "Gus" Grissom, a native of Mitchell, Indiana, was the first American to make two trips into space.

Songwriter Cole Porter, born in Peru, Indiana, provided words and music for more than 30 Broadway and Hollywood hits, including *Kiss Me Kate* and *Anything Goes*.

Lincoln Boyhood National Memorial.

Wyandotte Cave.

OF SPECIAL INTEREST

NEAR LINCOLN CITY: *Lincoln Boyhood National Memorial*
Here is the farm where Abraham Lincoln lived between the ages of 7 and 21; his mother's grave is on this site.

IN VINCENNES: *William Henry Harrison Home*
This brick building was Harrison's home while he was territorial governor of Indiana during the early 1800s.

NEAR LEAVENWORTH: *Wyandotte Cave*
This limestone cavern is one of the largest in the world, with 35 miles of passageways on 5 levels.

IN GREENFIELD: *James Whitcomb Riley Home*
A white frame house is preserved as it was when the beloved "Hoosier Poet" was growing up in the mid-19th century.

For more information write:
INDIANA DEPARTMENT OF COMMERCE
TOURISM DEVELOPMENT DIVISION
400 NORTH MERIDIAN STREET
INDIANAPOLIS, INDIANA 46204

FURTHER READING

Aylesworth, Thomas G. and Virginia L. *Indiana*. Bison Books, 1985.
Carpenter, Allan. *Indiana*, rev. ed. Childrens Press, 1979.
Dillon, Lowell I., and Lyon, E. E., eds. *Indiana: Crossroads of America*. Kendall/Hunt, 1978.
Hoover, Dwight W., and Rodman, Jane. *A Pictorial History of Indiana*. Indiana University Press, 1981.
Nolan, Jeanette. *Indiana*. Coward, McCann & Geoghegan, 1969.
Peckham, Howard H. *Indiana: A Bicentennial History*. Norton, 1978.

Jewel-like lights outlining the five-mile span of the
  mighty Mackinac Bridge.
The deafening cheers of 100,000 Maize and Blue fans
  at a football game in Ann Arbor.
Turbulent water plunging over Tahquamenon Falls
  near Newberry.
Young people dressed in colorful Dutch costumes for
  the annual Tulip Festival.
Sleek dairy cattle grazing in peaceful pastures near
  Lansing.
The smell of toasting grain in the air at Battle Creek.

Let's Discover
Michigan

MICHIGAN
At a Glance

Capital: Lansing

Major Crops: Corn, winter wheat, soybeans, oats, fruit
Major Industries: Automobiles, machine tools, food processing

State Flag

Size: 58,216 square miles (23rd largest)
Population: 9,075,000 (8th largest)

State Flower:
Apple Blossom

State Bird: Robin

N
△

★ State Capital
● Cities or towns
■ OF SPECIAL INTEREST

Keweenaw Bay

LAKE SUPERIOR

Whitefish Bay

SAULT SAINTE MARIE

OTTAWA NATIONAL FOREST

HIAWATHA NATIONAL FOREST

HIAWATHA NATIONAL FOREST

WISCONSIN

Green Bay

MACKINAW CITY

LAKE HURON

HURON NATIONAL FOREST

MICHIGAN

Saginaw Bay

MANISTEE NATIONAL FOREST

Bay City

Saginaw

WISCONSIN

LAKE MICHIGAN

Muskegon

Grand Rapids

Wyoming

★**Lansing**

Flint

Port Huron

Lake Saint Clair

Holland

Pontiac

Detroit

Battle Creek

ILLINOIS

Kalamazoo

Jackson

Ann Arbor

■DEARBORN

Adrian

Monroe

LAKE ERIE

INDIANA

OHIO

0   20   60   100 Miles
0   20   60   100   150 Kilometres

25

The Land

The Lower Peninsula of Michigan is bordered on the west by Lake Michigan; on the north by Lakes Michigan and Huron; on the east by Lakes Huron and Erie and the Canadian province of Ontario; and on the south by Indiana and Ohio. The Upper Peninsula is bounded on the west and north by Lake Superior, on the east by Ontario, and on the south by Wisconsin and Lakes Michigan and Huron. There are two main land regions in the state: the Superior Upland and the Great Lakes Plains.

Most of Michigan is surrounded by four of the five Great Lakes. The state's coastline includes protected bays and capes that jut into Lakes Michigan, Superior, Huron, and Erie.

All of Michigan's rivers flow into the Great Lakes. The state's largest rivers are located in the Lower Peninsula.

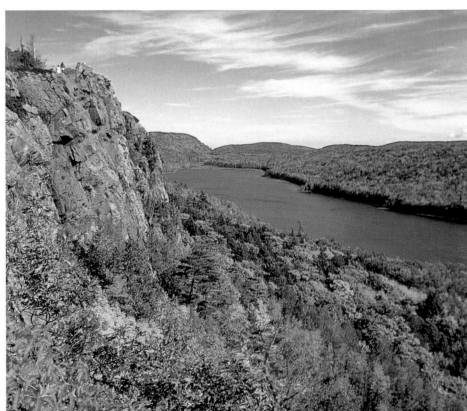

Most of Michigan's sandy beaches are along the coast of the Lower Peninsula. Miles of shoreline provide ample opportunities for recreation and contribute to the state's economy.

The Superior Upland covers the western half of the Upper Peninsula and is part of a larger land area shared with Wisconsin and Minnesota. Most of the Upland consists of a rugged plateau that ranges from 600 to 2,000 feet above sea level. The Porcupine Mountains are here, most of them covered with forests. Iron and copper are mined in the region, and forestry and forest products are other chief industries.

The Great Lakes Plains cover the rest of the state—the eastern Upper Peninsula and all of the Lower Peninsula. This is part of a region that stretches along the Great Lakes from Wisconsin to Ohio. Much of the land is flat, but hills occur in some parts of it. The shores of Lake Michigan have many high bluffs and sand dunes. In the Upper Peninsula, forest products and stone quarrying are major industries. The Lower Peninsula, where most of the farming is done, has richer soil and a longer growing season. Wheat, vegetables, fruit, potatoes, corn, poultry, and beef and dairy cattle are raised here. The region also has oil and natural gas wells.

Michigan's rugged Upper Peninsula has a landscape of rocky hills, rushing streams, and some 150 dramatic waterfalls.

The Great Lakes shoreline of Michigan is 3,288 miles long—longer than that of any other inland state. The chief rivers of the Upper Peninsula are the Escanaba, Manistique, Menominee, Ontonagon, Sturgeon, Tahquamenon, and Whitefish, many of which have beautiful waterfalls.

In the Lower Peninsula are the Au Sable, Clinton, Grand, Huron, Kalamazoo, St. Joseph, and other rivers. Important commercial waterways include the Detroit, St. Clair, and St. Mary's Rivers. This well-watered state has more than 11,000 lakes.

Variations in climate between the Upper and Lower Peninsulas are substantial. In the Upper Peninsula, the average January temperature is about 15 degrees Fahrenheit, and the average July temperature 64 degrees F. But Detroit, in the Lower Peninsula, has an average January temperature of 26 degrees F. and a July average of 74 degrees F. Rainfall amounts to about 30 inches annually, well dispersed through the year. Winter often brings heavy snows, especially in the Upper Peninsula, which has recorded annual snowfalls of more than 50 feet.

A picturesque winter scene on a Michigan farm. Winters are often harsh, with annual snowfall sometimes mounting to 50 feet in the Upper Peninsula.

A vest crafted by the Chippewa Indians, who were among the first inhabitants of Michigan's Upper Peninsula.

The History

When the first Europeans arrived in what was to become Michigan, some 15,000 Indians were living there—most of them belonging to tribes of the Algonquian language group. In the Upper Peninsula, the Chippewa and Menominee were the most numerous inhabitants. In the Lower Peninsula were the Miami, the Ottawa, the Potawatomi, and others. The Wyandot, members of the Iroquoian language group, lived near what is now Detroit.

Probably the first European to visit Michigan was the French explorer Étienne Brûlé, who explored the Upper Peninsula after landing at Sault Ste. Marie in 1618. He had been sent from Quebec by Samuel de Champlain, the governor of New France (now Canada). Within a few years, French fur traders and trappers were making their way to Michigan.

Champlain sent another explorer, Jean Nicolet, to the region in 1634. Nicolet was looking for a route to the Pacific Ocean, and he sailed through the Straits of Mackinac, between the Upper and Lower Peninsulas, and explored parts of the Upper Peninsula. In 1660 the first mission in the area was founded at Keweenaw Bay by the Jesuit René Ménard. Eight years later Sault Ste. Marie became Michigan's first permanent non-Indian settlement, established by the famous explorer-priest Jacques Marquette. In 1671 another settlement, which would become the town of St. Ignace, was established on the northernmost point of land between Lakes Michigan and Huron. The Indians called the place Michilimackinac. Later it became the British Fort Mackinac because of its strategic location.

The British built Fort Mackinac on Mackinac Island, between the Upper and Lower Peninsulas, in the 1700s. Its strategic location made it a vital military outpost for British and, later, American troops.

Naval commander Oliver Hazard Perry led an American flotilla to victory in the Battle of Lake Erie, during the War of 1812, thus restoring U.S. control of Lake Erie and the area around it. When Perry's ship, the *Lawrence*, was disabled in the engagement, he transferred his flag to the *Niagara* and compelled the British to surrender. This was the occasion of his famous message, "We have met the enemy and they are ours."

For the French, the lure of the Michigan forest was furs, and within a few years the annual shipment of pelts exceeded 200,000. By 1700 the French had built forts, missions, and trading posts at several places in both peninsulas. In 1701 Fort Pontchartrain, now the city of Detroit, was founded by Antoine Cadillac.

During this period, the British and the French were vying for control of North America. The Indians sided with the French, continuing to resist white incursions into their territory. The British were massacred at Fort Mackinac in 1763. That same year, an army of some 900 Indians, led by Chief Pontiac, besieged Detroit for nearly six month, but the rebellion fizzled out in the fall. When the French and Indian Wars ended, Britain won most of the French holdings in North America.

During the Revolutionary War, which began in 1775, British troops from Detroit enlisted Indian aid to raid some American settlements. Although the war ended in 1783, when the Michigan area became part of the United States, the British did not surrender Detroit and Fort Mackinac until 1796.

What is now Michigan became part of the Northwest Territory in 1787 and of the Indiana Territory in 1800. Five years later Congress created the Territory of Michigan, which did not include the western section of the Upper Peninsula. During the War of 1812, the British recaptured Detroit and Fort Mackinac. But the Americans regained these two outposts in 1813 and 1814, respectively.

After the Erie Canal opened in 1825, linking the Great Lakes with the Atlantic Ocean, a steady stream of settlers moved into Michigan, chiefly from New England and New York. Michigan, including the entire Upper Peninsula, became the 26th state on January 26, 1837.

Iron-ore mining began in 1845, and many miners and prospectors came to the Upper Peninsula. When construction of the Soo Canals was completed in 1855, mine owners were able to ship ore from western Michigan to the iron and steel centers in the lower Great Lakes states.

A view of Detroit in 1820, when Michigan's population was growing rapidly as a result of territorial status and the defeat of Indian claims to the land. Five years later, completion of the Erie Canal would bring new settlers from the East.

During the Civil War, many Michiganders fought on the Union side. One of their crack units, the Fourth Michigan Cavalry, led by George Armstrong Custer, captured Confederate president Jefferson Davis in 1865.

After the Civil War, lumber became a big business in Michigan. This, in turn, fostered the furniture industry, of which Grand Rapids became the center. At the turn of the century, Michigan made its move toward becoming the automobile capital of the world when Ransom E. Olds founded the Olds Motor Works in Detroit in 1899. Oldsmobiles were being mass-produced by 1901. Two years later, Henry Ford organized the Ford Motor Company in Detroit.

When the United States entered World War I in 1917, the auto companies built trucks, armored vehicles, airplane engines, and other military products. Postwar improvements to Michigan's highway system brought many tourists to Mackinac Island and other beautiful resorts. But Michigan faced serious problems during the Great Depression of the 1930s. Hundreds of thousands of workers in the automobile industry lost their jobs, since a car was still a luxury at the time. Copper mining went into a decline because of the expense of extracting the deeply buried ore.

Automobile pioneer Henry Ford, a native of Dearborn, was instrumental in making Michigan the automobile capital of the nation. Ford's company was the first to successfully mass-produce a simple, inexpensive car that the public could afford. His four-cylinder Model T revolutionized the industry and made the Ford Motor Company one of the most successful in the world.

During World War II, Michigan reassumed its role as a center for the manufacture of airplanes, ships, tanks, and other military equipment. In fact, the entire automobile industry made nothing but these products between 1941 and 1945. Prosperity continued in the postwar years. In 1957 the great five-mile bridge across the Straits of Mackinac connected the two peninsulas. Five years later, the International Bridge to Canada opened at Sault Ste. Marie. Petroleum and natural gas reserves were developed.

Michigan's economic development has had a cyclic pattern. First there were the trees that created a great lumber industry; these were rapidly depleted. The copper and iron-ore mines followed, and they too fell into a decline. Michigan's primary mineral products today are cement, salt, crushed stone, sand, and gravel. Finally, the automobile industry, once the mainstay of the state's prosperity, has experienced difficulties with the high cost of labor and low-cost cars imported from abroad. Diversified industries like chemicals, plastics, and food have helped close the gap. The St. Lawrence Seaway made some Michigan cities international ports, which strengthened commerce, and tourism had become a $3 billion business by the early 1980s.

The St. Lawrence Seaway, completed in 1959, has played a large part in Michigan's economic prosperity. It made international ports of many Michigan cities, opening them to trade with business around the world.

The sixth largest city in the nation, Detroit is Michigan's primary business, cultural, and educational center.

The first schools in Michigan were established by Roman Catholic missionaries to the Indians in the 1600s. In 1798 the first schools to teach both white and Indian children were established in Detroit by Father Gabriel Richard. The first public-school law was passed in 1809, and in 1837 a state-wide system of public education was approved by the legislature. Even before Michigan became a state in 1837, there were three institutions of higher education in the territory: the University of Michigan (1817), Kalamazoo College (1833), and Albion College (1835). When the Civil War began in 1861, six more colleges and universities had been established: Hillsdale College (1844), Olivet College (1844), Adrian College (1845), Eastern Michigan University (1849), Hope College (1851), and Michigan State University (1855). Eastern Michigan University was the first state teachers college west of New York, and Michigan State University was the first state school to offer agricultural courses for credit.

Gerald R. Ford, the 38th president of the United States, spent much of his political life representing Michigan in Congress. As vice-president, he assumed the presidency when Richard Nixon resigned in 1974.

The People

More than 70 percent of Michigan's residents live in towns and cities, including Detroit, Flint, and Grand Rapids. About 93 percent of them were born in the United States. Of those born in other countries, most are from Canada. European immigrants came from Poland, Italy, England, Germany, Russia, Scotland, and the Netherlands. The largest religious group in the state is made up of Roman Catholics. Other important denominations include the Episcopal, Lutheran, Methodist, and Presbyterian.

Many distinguished Americans have come from Michigan. Nobel laureate and diplomat Ralph Bunche was born in Detroit. Automobile pioneer and industrialist Henry Ford came from Wayne County, and W. K. Kellogg, of breakfast-cereal fame, was a native of Battle Creek. Charles A. Lindbergh, the first person to fly the Atlantic Ocean alone, came from Detroit.

In the field of popular music, Michigan has produced some of the leaders. Aretha Franklin, Diana Ross, and Della Reese are natives of Detroit. Madonna (Ciccone) was born in Bay City, and Stevie Wonder is from Saginaw. Actors and actresses from Michigan include Ellen Burstyn, Harry Morgan, Tom Selleck, Lily Tomlin, and Robert Wagner (all from Detroit), Danny Thomas (Deerfield), and Lee Majors (Wyandotte). The Academy Award-winning film director Francis Ford Coppola was born in Detroit.

United Nations mediator and educator Ralph Bunche, the grandson of a slave, was born in Detroit and orphaned at the age of 13. His successful negotiation of agreements between Israel and the Arab states in 1949 won him the Nobel Peace Prize, awarded in 1950.

Greenfield Village and the Henry Ford Museum.

Dutch Village.

OF SPECIAL INTEREST

IN DEARBORN: *Greenfield Village and the Henry Ford Museum*
The village consists of historic buildings restored by Henry Ford, including the Edison Institute School and buildings associated with Abraham Lincoln, educator William H. McGuffey, composer Stephen Foster and others. The Henry Ford Museum is next to the village.

AT SAULT STE. MARIE: *Soo Canals*
Huge locks permit ships to travel between Lakes Huron and Superior on the U.S.-Canadian border.

IN MACKINAW CITY: *Fort Michilimackinac*
This reconstruction of the British fort built in the 1700s includes the commander's house and Ste. Anne's Jesuit Church.

NEAR HOLLAND: *Dutch Village*
Buildings of Dutch design, canals, windmills, and street organs recall the heritage of industrious Dutch settlers. Holland holds a week-long Tulip Festival each May.

For more information write:
THE TRAVEL BUREAU
MICHIGAN DEPARTMENT OF COMMERCE
BOX 30226
LANSING, MICHIGAN 48909

FURTHER READING

Bailey, Bernadine. *Picture Book of Michigan*, rev. ed. Whitman, 1967.
Bald, Frederick Clever. *Michigan in Four Centuries*, rev. ed. Harper & Row, 1961.
Carpenter, Allan. *Michigan*, rev. ed. Childrens Press, 1978.
Catton, Bruce. *Michigan: A Bicentennial History.* Norton, 1976.
Dunbar, Willis F. *Michigan: A History of the Wolverine State*, rev. ed. Eerdmans, 1980.
Fradin, Dennis B. *Michigan in Words and Pictures.* Childrens Press, 1980.

Spinnakers billowing aboard sailing sloops on Lake Erie.

A feeling for antiquity at the Great Serpent Mound near Hillsboro.

The thrill of the finish line at the Soap Box Derby in Akron.

Sparkling winter snow blanketing a farm in the Till Plains region.

Thousands of Buckeyes cheering their Reds in Cincinnati's Riverfront Stadium.

A gleaming sunset reflected in the waters of the Ohio River near Gallipolis.

Let's Discover
Ohio

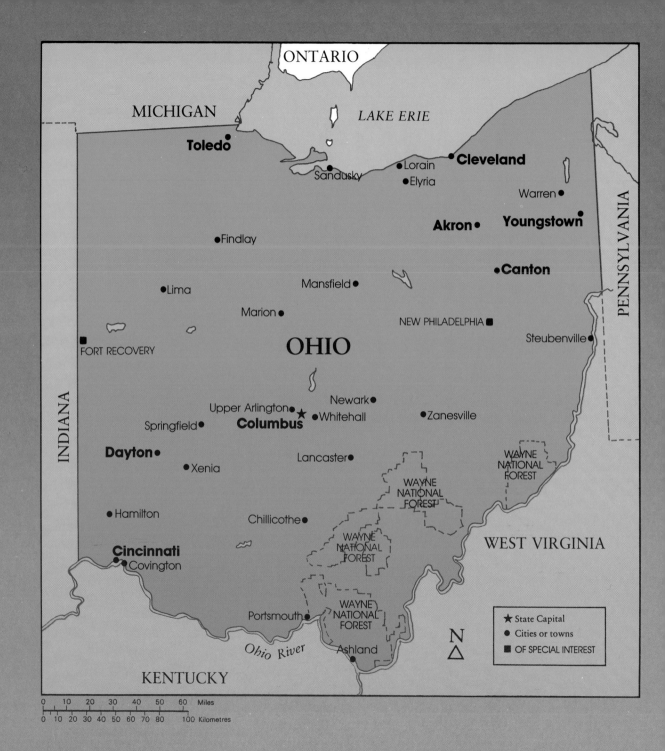

OHIO
At a Glance

State Flag

Capital: Columbus

Major Industries: Transportation equipment, machinery, metal products

Major Crops: Corn, hay, winter wheat, oats, soybeans

State Bird: Cardinal

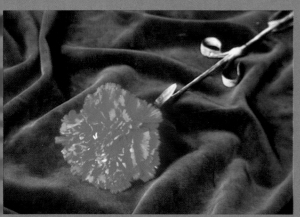

State Flower: Scarlet Carnation

Size: 41,222 square miles (35th largest)

Population: 10,752,000 (7th largest)

45

Ohio is bounded on the west by Indiana, on the north by Michigan and Lake Erie, on the east by Pennsylvania and West Virginia, and on the south by West Virginia and Kentucky. There are four main land regions in the state, formed primarily by the Ice Age glaciers. They are the Great Lakes Plains, the Till Plains, the Appalachian Plateau, and the Bluegrass Region.

The Great Lakes Plains lie along the northern border of Ohio and are part of a larger area that borders the Great Lakes. These level plains are broken by a few low sandy ridges along Lake Erie. The region has fertile soil, and fruits and vegetables are its chief crops. It is also a populous area of large cities, lake ports, and industrial complexes.

The Till Plains, part of the great Midwestern Corn Belt, are located in western Ohio. There are some hills here in what is one of the nation's most fertile farming areas. Grain and livestock are raised in the Till Plains, which also contain a few industrial cities.

While much of Ohio is highly industrialized, agriculture remains an important part of the state's economy. Many of the largest farms can be found in the northwest and central portions of the state.

Southwestern Ohio is an extension of the Kentucky Bluegrass Region. This area is well suited to horse raising and the cultivation of tobacco, corn, and wheat.

The Appalachian Plateau is located in eastern Ohio. The southern part of the area, the only section not glaciated, is rugged country, where most of the soil is not suitable for farming. But in the north, the soil produces both crops and good pasturage for dairy cows.

The Bluegrass Region is a small triangular area in southwestern Ohio that extends from Kentucky's Bluegrass Region. Tobacco is grown here. Corn, wheat, and beef cattle are other farm products of the region.

Ohio's shoreline extends for 312 miles along Lake Erie. The state has some 44,000 miles of rivers and streams, of which the Ohio is the most important. Other major waterways are the Miami, Hocking, Muskingum, Scioto, Cayahoga, Maumee, Sandusky, and Vermilion Rivers. Ohio has more than 2,500 lakes with an area larger than two acres.

Ohio's climate is continental, or mid-American, with from 35 to 39 inches of rainfall throughout the year, fairly well distributed over the state. Cleveland, in the north, has an average January temperature of 28 degrees Fahrenheit and a July average of 71 degrees F. Cincinnati, in the south, has a January average of 33 degrees F. and a July average of 76 degrees F. In the snow belt along the shore of Lake Erie, heavy winter snowfalls are likely to occur. The Cincinnati area has the state's hottest summer weather.

Southeastern Ohio has a rugged landscape dotted with many small rivers and lakes, including Lake Vesuvius, seen here.

The History

Paleo-Indians lived in what is now Ohio more than 5,000 years ago. Later groups, known to us as Mound Builders, left more than 6,000 burial mounds, forts, and other earthworks throughout the state, the products of a high form of civilization. These cultures flourished from about 1400 B.C. to A.D. 500.

The first Europeans to arrive encountered the Delaware, Miami, Shawnee, Huron (or Wyandot), and other tribes. The first non-Indian to visit the Ohio area was probably the French explorer Robert Cavelier (La Salle), who arrived in 1670. The French based their claim to the entire Northwest on his explorations. The British also claimed these lands, which they viewed as extensions of their Eastern colonies. The British Ohio Company of Virginia sent Christopher Gist to explore the upper Ohio River Valley in 1750, with a view toward colonizing the area. British soldiers and explorers from the Atlantic Seaboard colonies built wilderness garrisons (some of which would become cities) and held the land against the French in a long series of struggles—the French and Indian Wars—that ended in 1763. France gave up its claims to all lands as far west as the Mississippi River in a treaty signed that year.

A Moravian religious settlement named Schoenbrunn, near present-day New Philadelphia, had been established in 1772. But it disbanded a few years later because of Revolutionary War battles nearby. In 1780 George Rogers Clark defeated Indian allies of the British in the Battle of Piqua, near what is now Springfield. Clark's frontier campaigns helped win the region for the United States.

After the American Revolution, Ohio was included in the Northwest Territory (roughly the present area of the Midwest), and settlement began. The first permanent non-Indian settlement was at Marietta, near the Ohio River, in 1788. Cincinnati was founded the same year. The area began to fill with settlers, as Revolutionary War

Revolutionary War hero General Rufus Putnam was superintendent of the Ohio Company of Associates, a group formed in the late 1780s to purchase large tracts of land in the Ohio country. The company bought 1,500,000 acres in southeastern Ohio for about 75 cents per acre and founded the state's first permanent non-Indian settlement, the town of Marietta.

veterans received its land in payment for their services. The Indians had resisted encroachments on their territory since the 1760s, when Chief Pontiac led an unsuccessful uprising against the British. After the Revolution, resistance continued under the leadership of Miami chief Little Turtle and others. General Anthony Wayne dealt a death blow to the Indian cause at the Battle of Fallen Timbers, near present-day Toledo, in 1794.

Twelve years after the first settlement, and three years before Ohio became a state, the area had a population of more than 45,000—chiefly immigrants from New England, Pennsylvania, and Kentucky. Among them was a man named John Chapman, whose nickname was "Johnny Appleseed." His passion for orchards gave the fields cut from the forests a springtime pattern of flowering trees, and still gives Ohio a high rank among apple-producing states.

Ohio became the 17th state in the Union in 1803, with Chillicothe as its capital. The capital was moved to Zanesville in 1810, then back to Chillicothe in 1812. Finally, Columbus became the capital in 1816.

During the War of 1812 with Great Britain, one of the most important battles took place off the Ohio shore on Lake Erie. Commodore Oliver H. Perry sailed from Put-in-Bay at South Bass Island to defeat the British fleet in the Battle of Lake Erie on September 10, 1813.

The Erie Canal across New York from Lake Erie opened in 1825, offering a new and easy route for settlement of Ohio and the West. Thousands of families moved in from northern New York and New England. European immigrants, especially Germans, arrived in great numbers, and by 1830 there were almost a million people in the state. Transportation continued to improve with completion of the Ohio and Erie Canal from Cleveland to Portsmouth in 1832. And the Miami and Erie Canal from Toledo to Cincinnati opened in 1845. Railroads reached Ohio from the East, increasing population and prosperity. Mills and factories were built.

The city of Cleveland in 1850. The mid-19th century was a time of great growth for Ohio, particularly in the north, where successful drainage projects opened up new land for farming.

Ohioans had mixed feelings about the issue of slavery: many were active abolitionists, while others sympathized with the South. But during the Civil War, which began in 1861, some 345,000 men responded to Union calls for volunteers—more than twice the state's quota. Ohio also provided the Union's key commanders: Generals Ulysses S. Grant, William T. Sherman, and Philip H. Sheridan. The only important military action within Ohio during the Civil War occurred when Confederate cavalrymen called Morgan's Raiders crossed into the state from Indiana. They were captured with their leader, General John Hunt Morgan, in Columbiana County, but Morgan escaped later and returned to the South.

Morgan's Raid, in 1863, was the only major penetration into Ohio by Confederate troops during the Civil War. After the unsuccessful attack, Confederate cavalry leader John Hunt Morgan and his men were imprisoned.

After the Civil War ended, Ohio's abundant natural resources and its strategic position between two of the country's principal waterways—Lake Erie on the north and the Ohio River on the south—paved the way for rapid industrialization and growth. Shipping and farming increased. In 1869 the Cincinnati Red Stockings (now the Reds) became the first professional baseball team, and rubber-products production was started in Akron by Benjamin F. Goodyear in 1870.

During World War I, which the United States entered in 1917, about 225,000 Buckeyes served in the armed forces, and the state produced vast amounts of war materials. The 1920s were a time of growth in Ohio, as many towns became cities, and barges loaded with coal and iron ore plied Lake Erie. But when the Great Depression of the 1930s began, many factory workers became unemployed as a result of plant closings. Ohio farmers lost their land when farm prices dropped.

Harvey Firestone, born in Columbiana, Ohio, founded the Firestone Tire and Rubber Company in Akron in 1900. The balloon tire he produced soon became an industry standard, and his successful business provided employment for thousands of Ohio workers.

During World War II, about 840,000 Ohioans were in the armed forces. Steel, tires, and other goods needed for the military made Ohio one of the top four states in contracts awarded for wartime industries. Aircraft, ships, and weapons rolled from Ohio assembly lines.

After the war ended in 1945, Ohio became one of the most important states in the development of atomic energy for peacetime use. The Ohio Turnpike, opened in 1955, stretched across the 241-mile width of northern Ohio.

Today, Ohio's industrial growth is still running at a strong pace. New industries are attracted by the state's four major ports, and there are international airports at Cleveland, Dayton, Cincinnati, and Columbus. Ohio has more large metropolitan areas than any other state. Ohioans are justifiably proud of their excellent state park system, their numerous tree-shaded towns, and their "Queen City," Cincinnati.

The first school in Ohio opened in 1773 at Schoenbrunn, near present-day New Philadelphia. It was set up by a Moravian missionary, David Zeisberger, to teach Indian children of the region. The public-school system of Ohio began in 1825, and public high schools were established from 1853 onward. The first institution of higher education in Ohio was Marietta College, which was founded in 1797. The second was Ohio University, which was established in 1804, just one year after statehood. Colleges and universities proliferated, and by the beginning of the Civil War in 1861, Ohio had 24 more of them, including Miami University (1809), the University of Cincinnati (1819), Kenyon College (1824), Western Reserve University (1826), The Athenaeum of Ohio (1829), Capital University (1830), Denison University (1831), Xavier University (1831), Oberlin College (1833), Muskingum College (1837), Ohio Wesleyan University (1842), Baldwin-Wallace College (1845), Wittenberg University (1845), Mount Union College (1846), and Otterbein College (1847).

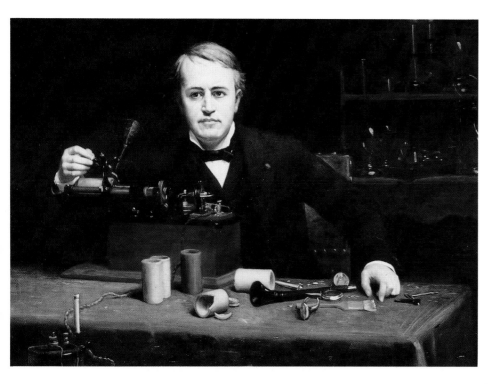

Inventor Thomas Alva Edison was born in Milan, Ohio. His numerous inventions included the incandescent light bulb, the phonograph, and one of the first successful motion-picture cameras.

The People

More than 73 percent of the people of Ohio live in towns and such cities as Cleveland, Cincinnati, Columbus, Dayton, Akron, and Toledo. About 95 percent of Ohioans were born in the United States. Most of those born in foreign countries came from Czechoslovakia, England, Germany, Hungary, Italy, and Poland. The largest religious group is the Roman Catholic community. Major Protestant denominations include the Disciples of Christ, Lutherans, Methodists, and Presbyterians.

Markswoman Annie Oakley, born in Darke County, Ohio, in 1860, starred in Buffalo Bill's Wild West Show for 17 years.

William Tecumseh Sherman, born in Lancaster, was one of the greatest Union generals of the Civil War.

Ohio has often been called "the Mother of Presidents," because seven of our chief executives were born in the Buckeye State. They were the 18th president, Ulysses S. Grant (Point Pleasant); the 19th president, Rutherford B. Hayes (Delaware); the 20th president, James A. Garfield (Orange); the 23rd president, Benjamin Harrison (near North Bend); the 25th president, William McKinley (Niles); the 27th president, William Howard Taft (Cincinnati); and the 29th president, Warren G. Harding (near Blooming Grove).

Far left:
Actress Lillian Gish, a native of Springfield, became a legend of the silver screen.

At left:
Clarence Darrow, renowned criminal lawyer and social reformer, was born near Kinsman, Ohio. He won fame in 1925 for his moving defense of John T. Scopes, who was charged with, and convicted of, teaching evolution in Tennessee's public schools, in what was called the "monkey trial."

OHIO: *Mother of Presidents*

Ulysses S. Grant a renowned Union general during the Civil War and the 18th president of the United states, was born in Point Pleasant.

Rutherford B. Hayes, born in Delaware, Ohio, was the 19th president of the United States.

James A Garfield, born in Orange, the 20th president.

North Bend native Benjamin Harrison, the 23rd president.

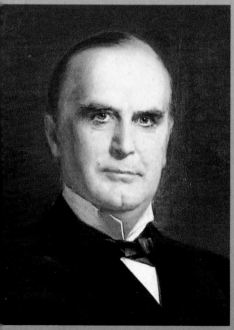

William McKinley, the 25th president, born in Niles.

William Taft, the 27th president, born in Cincinnati.

Warren G. Harding, the 29th president, born in Blooming Grove.

Two courageous Indian leaders were born in what would become Ohio—Tecumseh (near what is now Oldtown) and Pontiac (in northern Ohio). Tecumseh was a Shawnee political leader who envisioned a united Indian entity, and the Ottawa chief Pontiac led Pontiac's War against the British in 1763–64. Ohio has also produced such great inventors as Thomas Alva Edison (Milan), Harvey Firestone (Columbiana County), and Orville Wright (Dayton). Novelist Louis Bromfield, the author of *The Rains Came*, was born in Mansfield, and feminist leader Gloria Steinem is a native of Toledo. Championship golfer Jack Nicklaus came from Columbus and the astronaut who became a senator, John Glenn, was born in Cambridge.

Dayton native Orville Wright (left), and his brother Wilbur, who was born in Indiana, built the first successful airplane. In 1903, at Kitty Hawk, North Carolina, Orville made the first engine-powered flights in aviation history.

Far left:
John Glenn, born in Cambridge, was the first American astronaut to orbit the earth. He is now a U.S. senator from Ohio.

At left:
Astronaut Neil A. Armstrong, a native of Wapakoneta, Ohio, was the first man to set foot on the moon, in 1969.

In the field of popular music, Ohio has produced singer/actor Dean Martin (Steubenville), singer/actress Doris Day (Cincinnati), and composer Henry Mancini (Cleveland). Buckeye show-business personalities include circus sharpshooter Annie Oakley (Patterson Township) and television talk-show hosts Phil Donahue (Cleveland) and Jack Paar (Canton). Actors and actresses from Ohio include Lillian Gish (Springfield), *M*A*S*H* cast member Jamie Farr (Toledo), Paul Newman (Cleveland), Roy Rogers (Cincinnati), Martin Sheen (Dayton), and Debra Winger (Columbus). The inventive movie director Steven Spielberg was born in Cincinnati.

Schoenbrunn Village.

OF SPECIAL INTEREST

NEAR NEW PHILADELPHIA: *Schoenbrunn Village*
The Moravian mission founded in 1772 has been reconstructed here. It includes a
   replica of Ohio's first schoolhouse.

IN FORT RECOVERY: *Fort Recovery*
This is a reproduction of the fort built in 1793 by General "Mad Anthony" Wayne
   (nicknamed for his recklessness in battle) during the Indian wars in Ohio.

IN CLEVELAND: *Cleveland Health Education Museum*
One of the finest science museums in the world, it features displays and exhibits on
   the human body.

IN CINCINNATI: *Harriet Beecher Stowe Memorial*
The famous abolitionist novelist lived here from 1832 to 1850, when this was a
   meeting place for anti-slavery leaders, many of whom helped slaves escape
   into Canada by way of the Underground Railroad.

For more information write:
OHIO'S FOR YOU
OHIO OFFICE OF TRAVEL AND TOURISM
P.O. BOX 1001
COLUMBUS, OHIO 43216

FURTHER READING

Carpenter, Allan. *Ohio*, rev. ed. Children Press, 1979.
Collins, William R. *Ohio: The Buckeye State*, 6th ed. Prentice-Hall, 1980.
Crout, George C., and Rosenfelt, W. E. *Ohio: Its People and Culture*. Denison,
   1977.
Havinghurst, Walter. *Ohio: A Bicentennial History*. Norton, 1976.
Knepper, George W. *An Ohio Portrait*. Ohio Historical, Society, 1976.
Renick, Marion L. *Ohio*. Coward, McCann & Geoghegan, 1970.

INDEX

Numbers in italics refer to illustrations

63

Photo Credits/Acknowledgments

Photos on pages 5, 6–7, 8–9, 10, 11, 13, 16 (bottom), 17, 18, 20, courtesy of the Indiana Department of Commerce; pages 21, 22/23, 26, 27, 28, 29, 31, 36, 37, 40, courtesy of Michigan Travel Bureau; pages 41, 42–43, 46, 47, 62, courtesy of the Ohio Division of Travel and Tourism; page 45 (top left), James Kersell; pages 15, 19 (bottom), 32, 39, 53, 55, 56 (right), 58, 59, National Portrait Gallery; page 30, Museum of the American Indian; pages 34, 51, New York Public Library/Stokes Collection; pages 16 (top), 35, 38, 49, 52, 56 (left), 57 (right), 60 Library of Congress; pages 19 (top), 61, NASA.

Cover photograph courtesy of the Indiana Department of Commerce.

The Publisher would like to thank Susan L. Nelson and Hope Hartman of the Indiana Department of Commerce, Patty Jo Clause of the Michigan Department of Commerce, and Timothy J. Moore of the Ohio Department of Commerce for their gracious assistance in the preparation of this book.